D1025090

The Life Cycle of a
Turtle

by Lisa Trumbauer

Consulting Editor: Gail Saunders-Smith, Ph.D.

Consultant: Bob Fay, Animal Curator
Western North Carolina Nature Center
Asheville, North Carolina

Pebble Books

an imprint of Capstone Press
Mankato, Minnesota

Pebble Books are published by Capstone Press
151 Good Counsel Drive, P.O. Box 669, Mankato, Minnesota 56002
http://www.capstone-press.com

1 2 3 4 5 6 08 07 06 05 04 03

Library of Congress Cataloging-in-Publication Data
Trumbauer, Lisa, 1963–
    The life cycle of a turtle / by Lisa Trumbauer.
    p. cm.—(Life cycles)
    Summary: Describes the physical characteristics, habits, and stages of
development of turtles.
    Includes bibliographical references and index.
    ISBN 0-7368-2092-2 (hardcover)
    1. Turtles—Life cycles—Juvenile literature. [1. Turtles.] I. Title. II. Life cycles
(Mankato, Minn.)
QL666.C5 T78 2004
597.92—dc21   2002154680

Note to Parents and Teachers

The Life Cycles series supports national science standards related
to life science. This book describes and illustrates the life cycle of
an eastern painted turtle. The life cycles of other turtle species differ
slightly. The images support early readers in understanding the
text. The repetition of words and phrases helps early readers
learn new words. This book also introduces early readers to
subject-specific vocabulary words, which are defined in the Words
to Know section. Early readers may need assistance to read some
words and to use the Table of Contents, Words to Know, Read
More, Internet Sites, and Index/Word List sections of the book.

(Table of Contents

Photographs in this book show the life cycle of an eastern painted turtle.

day 1

4

Egg

A turtle begins life
as an egg.

3 months

egg tooth

6

Hatchling

A hatchling hatches from the egg. The hatchling slices the eggshell open with its egg tooth.

The hatchling grows.
Its soft shell hardens.
The hatchling takes
care of itself.

5 months

Young Turtle

The hatchling grows
into a young turtle.
It basks in the sun.

adult

Adult

The young turtle becomes an adult after four years. Some turtles can live more than 20 years.

A male turtle courts a female turtle. The two turtles mate.

The female turtle digs
a hole. She lays three
to six eggs in the hole.

The female turtle covers
the eggs with dirt.
She leaves the eggs.
The sun keeps the
eggs warm.

hatchling

eggs

young turtle

adult

The Life Cycle

The eggs are the start
of a new life cycle.

(Words to Know

bask—to lie or sit in the sunshine; turtles are reptiles; reptiles bask in the sun to keep warm.

court—to attract for mating

egg tooth—a tooth-like part that sticks out on a turtle's nose; the egg tooth falls off after the turtle hatches.

hatch—to break out of an eggshell; turtles grow inside an egg for about three months; it takes some turtles up to 12 hours to hatch out of an egg.

life cycle—the stages of life of an animal; the life cycle includes being born, growing up, having young, and dying.

mate—to join together to produce young

shell—the hard covering on the body of a turtle; a turtle's shell is made of two pieces.

(Read More

Fridell, Ron, and Patricia Walsh. *Life Cycle of a Turtle.* Heinemann First Library. Chicago: Heinemann Library, 2001.

Hipp, Andrew. *The Life Cycle of a Painted Turtle.* The Life Cycles Library. New York: PowerKids Press, 2002.

Rustad, Martha E. H. *Turtles.* All About Pets. Mankato, Minn.: Pebble Books, 2002.

(Internet Sites

Do you want to find out more about turtles? Let FactHound, our fact-finding hound dog, do the research for you!

Here's how:

1) Visit *http://www.facthound.com*

2) Type in the **Book ID** number: **0736820922**

3) Click on **FETCH IT**.

FactHound will fetch Internet sites picked by our editors just for you!

Index/Word List

Word Count: 119
Early-Intervention Level: 12

Editorial Credits
Sarah L. Schuette, editor; Kia Adams, series designer; Jennifer Schonborn, interior designer; Enoch Peterson, production designer; Kelly Garvin, photo researcher; Karen Risch, product planning editor

Photo Credits
Dwight R. Kuhn, all